SO-DFI-604

BILL MARVIN
The Restaurant Doctor™

Hospitality Masters Press
Gig Harbor, Washington

Copyright © 2000 by William R. Marvin.
All rights reserved

Printed and bound in the United States of America.

No part of this book may be reproduced or transmitted in any form or by any means, electronic or mechanical, including photocopying, recording, or by an information storage and retrieval system without permission in writing from the publisher. For information, please contact Hospitality Masters Press, Post Office Box 280, Gig Harbor, WA 98335-0280 USA.

An exception to the above conditions is hereby granted to a reviewer who may quote brief passages in a review to be printed in a magazine or newspaper. Exception is also granted to a trade association or other industry organization which may excerpt sections of no more than 300 words for inclusion in a non-commercial newsletter with the credit line: "Excerpted with permission from *59½ Money-Making Marketing Ideas: Gaining Volume Without Losing Your Shirt!* available from Hospitality Masters Press, Gig Harbor, Washington"

This publication is intended to provide accurate and authoritative information in regard to the subject matter covered. It is sold with the understanding that the publisher is not engaged in rendering legal, accounting or other professional services. If legal advice or other expert assistance is required, the services of a competent professional person should be sought.

ClickArt by T/Maker
Photo Page 145 – Copyright © Stegner Portraits, Colorado Springs, CO

Library of Congress Catalog Card Number: 99-067094

ISBN 0-9656262-8-8

ATTENTION ASSOCIATIONS AND MULTI-UNIT OPERATORS:
Quantity discounts are available on bulk purchases of this book for premiums, sales promotions, educational purposes or fund raising. Custom imprinting or book excerpts can also be created to fit specific needs.

For more information, please contact our Special Sales Department, Hospitality Masters Press, PO Box 280, Gig Harbor, WA 98335 (800) 767-1055, e-mail: masters@harbornet.com, Fax: (888) 767-1055 Outside North America, phone (253) 858-9255, Fax: (253) 851-6887.

59½ Money-Making Marketing Ideas
Gaining Volume Without Losing Your Shirt!

CONTENTS

Part 4
BE GUEST-FRIENDLY

Part 5
GIVE GUESTS SOMETHING TO TALK ABOUT

Part 6
DIFFERENTIATE YOURSELF FROM OTHER RESTAURANTS

APPENDIX

Introduction

Introduction

A few years ago I was conducting training programs in Northern Ireland. The question I was repeatedly asked was, "What do you think of the restaurants in Ireland?"

What I noticed was that the restaurants were only as good as they had to be to stay in business. Perhaps it was lack of strong competition or lack of a model for what was possible. Whatever the case, I had many good meals that could easily have been great, if only a few small points had been addressed.

It was easy to see in another culture, but when I returned to the United States, it occurred to me that it is really no different in our country.

3

"Good enough" seems to be good enough . . . until some new competition forces operators to raise their food and service to a higher level.

Well, that time has come!

Restaurant sales are growing steadily as a healthy economy makes for more disposable income. But the number of restaurants is increasing faster than either the population or dining dollars. In other words, the pie is getting bigger but there are more and more slices being taken out of it.

Competition is on the increase and many operators are facing deteriorating sales volumes for the first time in their professional careers.

The American business psyche seems to believe that we always have to do more volume than we did last year, so the erosion of profits creates a real dilemma, both financially and psychologically.

Shrinking market area

As more restaurants enter the market, the distance people are willing to drive is steadily declining.

Mike Hurst, owner of 15th Street Fisheries in Fort Lauderdale, Florida estimates that ten years ago, his guests came 15-20 miles for dinner. Today, he says, the majority of his diners live within 2½ miles of his restaurant and the radius is slowly tightening.

4

People will drive by two or three other restaurants to get to you but, unless you are a serious destination restaurant, they are not likely to drive past twenty or thirty other places. They don't have to!

Guest-based marketing

So your most realistic option to build sales has to come from guests who are already within the acceptable travel distance . . . and your dining room is full of them! The trick is to be able to get them to come back again and again . . . and that is the basis of what I call guest-based marketing.

Building volume from your existing customer base is less expensive and more effective than advertising because you already know who the people are and can reach them directly. By contrast, when you put an ad in the newspaper, 98% of the people who read it would not come to you on a bet – you are just too far away.

The following pages are full of hints on how to build volume from your existing customer base without losing your shirt in the process.

The ideas are taken from my popular seminar on the same subject and are excerpted from my past books, most notably **Guest-Based Marketing, 50 Tips to Improve Your Tips** and **Cashing In On Complaints.**

If you already have these books in your library, this small volume will be a mini refresher course. If you do not have them, and want to explore these ideas in more depth, you will find more information on books and materials on Page 148.

A word of caution

You will do better to understand the thinking behind the ideas presented here than to blindly adopt them. Not every suggestion is appropriate for every restaurant (and implementing **all** of them is totally inappropriate for **any** operation!)

The trick is to adapt, not adopt. If you grasp the premise behind the idea and the principles that make it work, you will be able to identify and implement your own unique approach.

Get busy

It is time to raise the bar. "Good enough" is no longer acceptable if you hope to survive and prosper in the new marketplace. I know everyone is doing the best they can at the moment, but doing the best you can is materially different from being as good as you can be . . . and better than you have to be.

Why settle for good if you can be great? Do it now before your competition discovers these ideas!

Bill Marvin
The Restaurant Doctor™

Part 1

Increase
Frequency

1

Build loyalty,
not the check average

How would you like a 50% sales increase? (Who wouldn't?) For the sake of illustration, let's say your typical guest comes in twice a month and spends ten dollars. What are your options?

Option 1: Increase the check average
You could try to increase your average check to $15 and hope that people would still come in as often as they did before. You might be able to pull this off but I wouldn't bet on it. Most operators tell me their guests have a certain amount they are comfortable spending and pressure to increase the per person expenditure could result in lowered guest counts. Raising the average check is not likely to work.

9

Option 2: Advertise

How about an aggressive promotion campaign? Well, you know that advertising can be expensive and every cost you add raises the sales required to net out a 50% increase. Besides, the odds of coming up with a campaign that would produce a consistent 50% sales increase are also quite slim. Promotion is usually not a viable answer.

Option 3: Increase frequency

What are the odds that you could treat your guests in such a way that instead of coming in twice a month, they would come in three times a month?

One more visit a month would easily provide that 50% sales increase . . . without any increase in the check average and without any increased pressure on the guests or your service staff! If you can give your guests such a good experience that they come to you instead of patronizing your competition, you cannot help but increase your volume.

You see how it works? A 50% sales increase seems impossible, but getting guests to come back one more time a month seems quite reasonable . . . and it is! After all, they are eating **somewhere,** why shouldn't it be with you?

Don't get me wrong – if a guest wants to spend more money, I have no problem taking it! But it is time we stopped having such fixation on how much

10

our guests spend on each visit and put our energy toward increasing the number of times they visit!

Higher checks are OK, but . . .
There is another problem: guest expectations rise with the check average . . . but they rise faster! This means that a two-dollar increase in the average check may bring about a four-dollar increase in the expectations of your guests.

You may be able to get the extra two bucks, but if you cannot deliver the extra $4 worth of experience, you risk alienating your guests. Be sure you don't upsell yourself down the river!

Peaceful coexistence
The two are not necessarily incompatible. It is possible to build both repeat patronage **and** the check average. However, I place the focus on the human side of the equation because foodservice is a business based on personal relationships.

I do not believe that success in building the average per person sale will guarantee guest loyalty or repeat patronage nor will it necessarily sustain long term sales growth.

On the other hand, I firmly believe that success in building guest loyalty and repeat patronage will always increase total revenue and sustain it over the long term.

11

2

Invite guests to return

If you accept that the safest way to build sales is by getting guests to return more often, you must also acknowledge that responsibility for implementing this idea falls primarily on your service staff.

The easiest way for the service staff to generate repeat visits is simply to invite guests to return, but they have to invite them back on a specific day for a specific reason.

"Y'all come back" is nice and friendly, but it isn't very likely to move people to action.

In general, the staff will generate more repeat business if they say something more targeted:

12

"Please come back this Thursday. We've got a fajita special that's a great deal. I'll be working that night and would really enjoy seeing you again."

If you are in a vacation area, and if, in the course of conversation, you find out where your guests are from and how long they are going to be in your area, you have the perfect opening for an invitation:

"You're headed home on Wednesday? I'd love to have you come back here for a going-away dinner on Tuesday night. I'll put together something really special for you."

Don't you think comments like these are more likely to generate a return visit than a simple "thank you?" (And yes, we always have to say "thank you.")

Festivals and special events
Another way to invite guests back on a specific day for a specific reason is to hold festivals and special events. These provide a natural, logical reason to invite guests to return.

Special events can either be a regular occurrence on a particular day of the week or month or something that only happens once a year. They can take a limitless variety of forms, but as a start, think of cigar dinners, wine-centered events, the restaurant's birthday, T-shirt Tuesday and charity fund raisers.

13

Festivals usually highlight a particular cuisine or a food product. They can be run on a specific day ("Thursday is Mexican Night") or for a specific period of time, usually a week or two.

Product festivals typically coincide with the height of the season for that particular product (a July strawberry festival, for example) when supplies are at their peak, quality is the highest and prices are at their lowest.

Whatever you do, "Come back next week for our salmon festival" sounds much more enticing than "Come back on Tuesday because it's slow and we need the business!"

3
Start a frequent diner plan

The premise behind customer loyalty programs or frequent diner plans (FDP's) is that people tend to do what they are rewarded for. What I most like about the concept is that the airlines have already done the basic consumer education on the concept.

The incentive for implementing an FDP is to encourage repeat patronage, thereby increasing sales volume.

The discount structure of the FDP also has the effect of lowering prices for members of the plan, which can be helpful in tourist markets where you want to keep prices up while keeping your operation affordable to the locals.

15

The "insider" appeal of a belonging to an FDP also helps members identify more closely with your restaurant, much as they would identify with a private club to which they belong.

Frequent flyers

Airline frequent flyer plans have done exactly what they were designed to do – created consumer loyalty and differentiated a product (airline seats) which would otherwise be a commodity. While they may be a tiger by the tail for the airlines, they have created a preference for one carrier over another.

Frequent diner plans reward guests for continued loyalty. Since the goal of increasing frequency is simply to get guests back one more time a month, including a frequent diner program in your plans can be extremely effective.

There are a number of variations on the FDP idea, all of which are based on rewarding guests for their return patronage, but the mechanics and logistics differ. There are three basic types:

Punch cards where a certain number of visits or a certain level of purchases earns a reward.

Point systems where each visit or purchase earns points which can be redeemed for various rewards.

Percentage of purchase programs where the guest earns a reward based on a specified percentage of their purchases.

16

There are pros and cons to each type of plan, but people will still do what they are rewarded for. If you want guests to come back more often, start rewarding them for doing it.

Part 2
Build Personal Connection

...between the staff and guests

4

Respect the power of presence

The secret to personal connection and personal service is **presence.**

Presence is a state of mind that is free from distraction. Your level of presence is the extent to which your mind is not occupied with thoughts unrelated to the project immediately at hand.

Lack of presence is obvious. Have you ever been talking to someone who was listening to you . . . and then suddenly they **weren't?** Didn't you know when their attention was elsewhere?

Or have you talked on the phone with a person who was doing something else as they spoke to you?

21

Even though you couldn't see them, wasn't their distraction apparent?

A distracted state of mind creates irritation in other people. It is incredibly annoying to talk to someone whose mind has wandered, yet we do it ourselves all the time. We think that the way to be efficient is to do several tasks at once. Wrong!

Presence and productivity

The truth is that you can only focus your attention on one thing at a time. For example, when you're talking with a person, there is nothing you can do at that instant about finishing the schedule or handling other chores on your list.

Presence is the secret to personal connection. It comes from dropping distractions, focusing on the task immediately at hand, then moving to the next project. Presence (lack of distraction) will enable you to be more in tune with others, accurately assess situations and deal with them effectively . . . the first time!

Presence and service

Ours is a business based on personal connection. In my service seminars, I point out that the reason guests tip 10% or 30% for doing essentially the same thing depends on the level of personal connection servers create with their guests.

When a server is distracted ("in the weeds"), there will be no personal connection. The guest will feel less served and tip accordingly.

Does this sound too easy? I watched a server go from making 11% and struggling to averaging more than 25% and cruising the next night.

A pizzeria manager who attended one of my programs called a few weeks later to say that over half his "people problems" had just disappeared!

In both cases, I asked what they were doing differently. Each essentially said, "I am just trying to *be* with people when I am with people."

This is the power of a clear mind when dealing with others. Presence is a potent quality that enhances the feeling of personal service and increases management effectiveness.

As you drop stray thoughts, you will naturally create more of a connection with the people in your life, become more expert with people, improve your productivity, reduce stress and increase enjoyment of your life both on and off the job.

23

5

Learn and use guests' names

The theme song to the television show "Cheers" said, "Sometimes you want to want to go where everybody knows your name."

Nothing sounds better to people than the respectful use of their own names. They also love that they are important enough to you that you remember who they are.

Do you have regular patrons – people who come in all the time? Do you know them all by name? I suspect you do. Most owners and managers get serious about recognizing regulars.

But if I was just hired as a member of your staff, is

24

there a **system** in place so that I would quickly start to know who these important people are . . . or do you leave it to chance?

Shari's, a regional coffee shop chain based in the Pacific Northwest, makes learning and knowing guests' names a part of their culture.

Servers who learn the names of 100 regulars get their name engraved on a plaque on the restaurant wall. There are servers in the company who know the names of 1400 regular guests! Do you think that patrons get the idea that they are important? Do you think that knowing the names of guests is an integral part of the Shari's culture? You bet it is!

How can you get names?
Have the greeter get the guest's name off the reservation list and pass it to the server. Ask a veteran co-worker for the name of a familiar-looking diner. Convention attendees often leave their name tags on! If a guest joins your frequent diner plan, you have all the information you could want.

When all else fails, ask them!

However you do it, learn the names of your regular guests, greet them by name when they arrive at the restaurant, welcome them by name when the server first gets to the table and use their names as often as appropriate during the meal.

25

A word of caution: don't address guests by their first names until and unless they give you permission to do so. Understand that this permission is granted on a person-by-person basis. Just because the guests asked you to use their first names does not automatically give everyone else on the staff the same privilege.

Repeated use of names will help everyone learn who your guests are . . . and your server's tips will reflect their additional effort.

6

Learn and use the names of your guests' children

People love people who love their kids and taking the time to learn the names of our guests' children can reap benefits in several ways:

First of all, it delights the parents.

Addressing the children by name is respectful and children are less likely to misbehave when they know that you know who they are.

7

Remember guests' preferences

Personal connection comes from taking care of each guest as a unique individual with distinctive needs and wants. This means that not all guests are treated exactly the same.

The golden rule does not apply. Treating guests the way *you* want to be treated will not necessarily assure success – you must treat people the way *they* want to be treated if you want them to feel personally served.

How can you treat people the way they want to be treated unless you notice what they need, ask how they want things and remember what they tell you?

For example, my wife has sensitive teeth, so she prefers water without ice. This does not seem too complicated, but the simple task of keeping her supplied with water often seems like a meal-long battle in some restaurants!

Bussers invariably bring a glass of ice water and we request a replacement without ice. It is disturbing to see how often bussers are upset by this simple request. It is even more disturbing when they continue to mindlessly refill her water glass with ice throughout the meal!

Hello! Was anybody paying attention? Does anybody care?

A world class restaurant would only need to be told once and they would remember it the next time we came in to dine! When a restaurant remembers, imagine how much more pleasant the dining experience is. When a restaurant remembers, imagine how important we feel to them!

All it takes to do this is the desire . . . and a system to support it. The Rattlesnake Club in Detroit keeps a biography card on their regular guests. The card includes everything the restaurant knows about the guest's needs, inclinations, patterns and desires.

If they have a seating preference, are allergic to certain foods or have a pet peeve, it is on the card.

After checking the night's reservations, the staff reviews the cards of the arriving guests so they will have the personal information fresh in their minds.

How much do *you* know about your regulars and how is that information made available within the organization?

8

Encourage call parties

Foodservice is a business based on personal connection and I firmly believe that people have more loyalty to people than they do to places. ("It's a great restaurant, but I go there because Bonnie always takes such good care of me.")

Think about it. Servers are essentially independent business people with a four- or five-table restaurant to run. The better they run their little operation, the more they can keep their tables full of people who want to be with them, the more money they make for themselves . . . and the restaurant!

Encouraging your servers to invite guests to ask for them on their return is a good way for the staff to build a regular following. Most servers probably have a few loyal patrons already and by supporting them in developing a personal connection, today's strangers can become tomorrow's regulars.

If you have ever followed a hairdresser around as she moved from salon to salon or waited fifteen minutes longer to have a particular barber cut your hair, you understand the idea at work here.

Personal connection is what drives the buying habit and makes you the restaurant of choice in an increasingly competitive market.

Randy Rayburn, owner of Sunset Grill in Nashville has doubled his volume . . . in a market with 50% more seats . . . and he has never calculated his average check!

He can easily figure it out, but he does not want to dignify the number with a calculation. He is only interested in two numbers: how many people walk in the door and "call parties" – how many people ask for each server by name.

Randy's premise is that the more people ask for a particular server, the better job that server is doing at creating a personal connection with the guests. He believes that ultimately, personal connection is what will drive sales volume.

32

How much money guests spend – and you can spend a hundred dollars as easily as you can spend ten in his restaurant – is of no consequence to him or anyone else on his staff. Just have a marvelous time and please come back soon!

In a market with 50% more seats, he has doubled his volume (and he was starting at $2.8 million.) Based on results, I would say he is right!

9

Have the chef serve the meal

Every so often, when you are into the back side of the dinner rush, have the chef bring the food out and serve it.

It will require a clean set of whites, of course, but imagine the reaction of a guest when the chef arrives at the table, presents the plate and says, "I just made this for you. I hope you enjoy it!"

10

Show sincere gratitude

Gratitude is powerful and no one gets all the appreciation they deserve. (Do you?)

Your guests have many options when it comes to dining out and they will tend to go where they feel their business is truly appreciated, where it matters to someone that they were there.

Showing gratitude means more than saying "thank you." In communication, the real message is always carried in the *feeling* behind the tone of voice you use – it is not just about your words.

(James Earl Jones could read the phone book and move people to tears because . . . that voice . . . !)

35

To convey a feeling of gratitude to your guests, stay in touch with the feeling of gratitude. When you do, it will come through in everything you say.

I suggest that if you have a picture that makes you feel good when you look at it – it could be a picture of your kids, your boat or the 17th green at Pebble Beach, it really doesn't matter – keep it on your desk. Servers might keep theirs in the service stand or tucked into their order pad.

When you feel yourself getting up tight and losing your sense of gratitude, take a quick break, pull out the picture and plug back into what is real. Let the warm feelings sweep over you and it will reset the feeling of appreciation.

Gratitude is a powerful way to help assure your guests' good will and future support. People give their business to people who appreciate their business.

11

Speak in complete sentences

We have a tendency to use shorthand when talking to guests.

"Smoking or non?"
"More rolls?"
"Coffee?"

While it is understandable, such shortcuts do not make your guests feel exceptionally well cared-for. Just adding one or two words to turn the phrase into a sentence can help create a higher level of service for your guests.

"Do you have a seating preference?"
"Can I bring you more rolls?"
" Would you like hot coffee?"

It works because having to speak in a complete sentence forces servers to think before they open their mouths. This, in turn, helps them to drop distracting thoughts which increases their presence. The guest's perception is a higher level of service.

Speaking in complete sentences will not take any more time and the result will be a higher sense of connection with the guest.

12

Make personal recommendations

Guests don't come to your place to be students of your menu. In many restaurants, trying to figure out the menu can be a career in itself! When your staff offers a personal recommendation, it is a personal gift of inside information for your guests and one which helps tie them closer together.

My advice to servers is to let their guests in on a secret. What looks particularly good today? What do **you** like? What do you want to have when **you** get off your shift? What do **you** think is the best thing on the menu? If you have an unusual little combination of things that you have created to break menu monotony, turn your guests on to it.

39

Don't try to guess what guests want – you can't do it – and don't develop a "one size fits all" spiel.

If a server goes on about the steak and I want a piece of fish, I will ask about the fish. You don't lose points with me by having an opinion . . . but have an opinion!

Never say "everything is good here." Even if it is true (and it should be), that statement is not particularly helpful as a recommendation.

Making personal recommendations is a safer way to build sales than the use of selling techniques.

I acknowledge that, done with style and grace, selling techniques can be effective . . . but most servers do not execute with style and grace. The result is that the guest feels manipulated. This is not the way to make them anxious to return to the restaurant.

The power of personal recommendation comes from the enthusiasm and sincerity with which it is made more than from the recommendation itself. I think people can only be enthusiastic and sincere about those items that they genuinely like.

To make valid personal recommendations, the staff must have tasted everything on the menu and watched how each item is prepared.

40

(This sounds so basic, but I once asked a waitress about a lobster dish on the menu. She said, "I don't know, they won't let us order it!")

The only way they will be able to make a valid personal recommendation is to speak from their personal experience rather than from a memorized script. Your servers must express themselves in the words that are most natural to them. Scripted communications will just put everyone – guests and servers alike – back into the manipulative world of sales techniques.

Recommending wine
To carry this idea a little farther, do you want the staff to recommend wines? If so, make sure they taste wines in combination with each menu item and come up with a personal favorite.

Often a wine will taste quite different with food than it will by itself. Since you typically sell the two together, it makes sense to taste them together. Discovering the nuances of wine and food and sharing these findings with guests can really be fun for everyone.

Don't get me wrong
By all means, servers should offer an opinion on appetizers, desserts, after-dinner drinks and all those other items that usually make it onto the suggestive selling list.

41

We need to give diners the opportunity to indulge themselves (if they want to) and to sample those items that set us apart from our competitors.

But to be effective, your staff must be sharing *their* excitement, not the management's – it is the *server's* enthusiasm and sincerity that makes a recommendation personal.

13

Reinforce guests' decisions

People are particularly vulnerable when they make a decision because nobody likes to make a mistake.

As an extreme example, imagine how you would feel if you ordered prime rib in a restaurant and the waiter rolled his eyes and started laughing! "Prime rib, huh? Are you really **sure** you want prime rib?"

If they order your favorite, **tell** them that it is your favorite. If what they order has been getting rave reviews from guests tonight, let them know. If they choose your best-selling item, pass that word along. If guests feel good about the decisions they make, they will be more likely to order additional items and try new things.

Even if what a guest selects is not your personal favorite, you can still reinforce their decision.

"That's one of our most popular items"
"Jack, one of our waiters, just raves about that!"
"You are really going to like that!"

You get the idea.

A few encouraging comments from you can help reassure your guests that they are making wise choices. That, in turn, will help keep them in a better mood.

When people are in a good mood, they are easier to get along with, spend more, tip better, have a better time and are more likely to return regularly.

14

Provide business cards
for everyone on your staff

When I opened my first restaurant in the mid '70s, one of my best decisions was having business cards printed for everyone on my staff. This inexpensive gesture did more to foster good will and connection with the restaurant than anything else I did.

Suddenly I had fifty people handing out business cards and extending personal invitations to dine at the restaurant. If the staff member signed their name on the card, it could be redeemed for a complimentary glass of wine or a dessert.

The staff did not take advantage of the privilege and genuinely appreciated the trust placed in them.

45

I had a motivated crew who was enthusiastically drumming up both sales volume and good will for the restaurant. Talk about effective marketing!

The team-building power of the cards is really quite simple – business cards are the mark of a professional in our society. I suspect that most managers would feel that they were not being taken seriously if they did not have business cards. Why would it be any different for the staff?

Depending on the complexity and colors of your artwork, 500 business cards could cost as little as ten dollars a person to print.

In a typical full service restaurant with about fifty full and part time workers, business cards for everybody would take an investment of less than five hundred dollars.

How much advertising can you buy for $500?

How much business do you think you might generate if you had fifty people handing out 500 cards apiece and extending personal invitations to dine at your restaurant?

15

Focus on guest delight

When it comes to service, everyone talks about the importance of making sure your guests are satisfied. While satisfaction is certainly better than dissatisfaction, in today's competitive market, satisfaction will not be enough to keep you growing and prospering over the long term.

As the foodservice pie gets sliced into more pieces, it is important to go beyond mere satisfaction and become memorable in the eyes of your guests. To be memorable, we must not only **meet** our guests' expectations, we must **exceed** them.

In other words, we must make sure our guests are **delighted!**

Delight differs from satisfaction

Diner delight is more important than good service because it has a different focus. As we already mentioned, the problem with talking to your staff about service is that it is too easy to define service from the perspective of the person providing it.

Manager: *"Did you give them good service?"*
Server: *"Yes, I did."*
Manager: *"Well then, why haven't they been back?"*

What makes delight so powerful is that it **cannot** be defined from the server's point of view. To see if the guest is delighted, you must look at the dining experience from the guest's perspective – the only point of view that really matters, anyway!

Focusing on delight forces you to see everything that happens in the restaurant through your guests' eyes and that will keep you more in touch with their dining experience.

It is important to understand that the hospitality is based on personal connection, not on technical execution.

Part 3
Build Personal
Connection

...with the
restaurant

16

Get a good start

Hospitality is about your ability to establish a warm, personal connection with your guests. To do that, you have to deal with your guests as individuals.

Get your greeters out from behind the podium. Better yet, get rid of the podium entirely. My idea of a great start to the meal is when, as the guest walks through the door, someone is moving toward them with a smile.

This does not require that the greeter be glued to the front door, just that someone maintain a sense of what is happening at the front door and head toward newly-arriving guests as soon as they enter the restaurant.

Time is of the essence. You have about 30 seconds from the time people first walk in the door to make eye contact, give them a smile and let **them** know that **you** know they are there.

If you are in the middle of something that can't wait, acknowledge them with smiling eye contact, finish your task quickly and take care of the guests. When guests sense that they are important to you as soon as they walk in the door, they will be in a much better mood for the rest of the meal.

This same principle applies everywhere in the restaurant. For example, when I opened my first restaurant in San Francisco, we were pouring more booze on Friday night than any other place in the City. It was not unusual for us to be two and three deep at the bar with people trying to get a drink.

We trained the bartenders to at least acknowledge those who were waiting. When guests knew that we had seen them, they waited patiently and were well-behaved. When we failed to make eye contact with those in the crowd, they pushed, jostled and kept shouting their orders to the bartender.

How long does a guest have to wait for the server to acknowledge them once they are seated? Guests just feel more comfortable if they know the server is aware that they are waiting. The longer they sit without contact, the more irritated they get.

You have about 60 seconds after people are seated to make an impression. Even if she is busy, the server should come to the table, STOP, focus her attention, smile, extend a friendly welcome and let the guests know she will be right back. That will buy about three minutes of slack.

If the server is too buried to start service within three minutes, she should ask for help. The longer guests wait, the worse their mood becomes, the harder they are to please and the lower the tip they are likely to leave.

People have many options when it comes to where they spend their money. Show them that they are important to you and they will spend it in your place!

17

Start a mug club

Do you sell draft beer? Do you want to sell more? Start a mug club!

When someone joins your mug club, they receive a personalized beer mug that you keep behind the bar for them. Whenever they come in, they drink from their own mugs and receive a special deal.

For example, if you sell a 12-ounce draft beer for two dollars, the mugs for club members might hold 14-16 ounces and sell for the same price.

The late Jim Casey implemented a mug club at his Casey's East Restaurant in Troy, New York several years ago. It cost $4 to join the club (which paid for

the mug and your first beer) after which members could refill their mugs for 25% less than an equal-sized pour cost nonmembers.

When he first started the idea, Jim figured that one or two dozen people might take him up on it but mug club membership rose to more than 100 in just three years and continues to grow.

The camaraderie among the members helps keep his bar full and Jim noticed that his regulars became a lot more regular when the program went into effect.

McGuire's Irish Pub in Pensacola, Florida has over 5000 members of their mug club, due mainly to the large number of vacationers who come to the area. McGuire's has mugs everywhere – on the ceiling, in wall racks and in every available corner. If you have a mug on the wall at McGuire's, you will probably stop there every time you are close to Pensacola!

Mug clubs do not have to be limited to beer. You could adapt the same idea to work with breakfast by finding a really great-looking coffee mug that can be personalized and a deal to make it interesting to "members."

How about a wine club where members receive a personalized crystal wine glass, the better to (more frequently) explore the finer wines from your cellar?

Regardless of their form, the premise behind mug clubs and their kind are similar:

1. The mugs, glasses, cups or whatever remains at the restaurant, typically on display, so the guests have to return to the property to use it.
2. The appearance of the vessel is so distinctive that it is obvious to the other guests in the room when it is being used, making the member feel privileged.
3. The container is personalized with the name of the member and (usually) the logo of the restaurant, the closer to tie the two together.
4. The club member receives a deal – usually either a lower price or more product at the same price – that is not available to nonmembers.

Oyster Club

Do you have an oyster bar? Start a club! Marc Valente, owner of Marc's restaurant in Wheatridge, Colorado instituted his Oyster Club several years ago. To become a member, guests must order (and pay for) 200 oysters at full price from the restaurant's oyster bar. He provides a tally card for this purpose.

Once a guest becomes an official member of the oyster club, their name is engraved on a brass plate and added to oyster club membership plaque. The membership card enables them to happy hour prices on oysters at any time. Marc reports nearly one thousand diners became oyster club members in the first five years of its existence.

You can start a club based on almost anything, but the goal is always the same – to cause your guests to identify more closely with your restaurant over the competition and to bring them back more often.

18

Create a Wall of Fame

The Wall of Fame is a way to recognize your regulars, usually by mounting their photo or their caricature on the wall of the restaurant.

If you choose to recognize someone this way, a few words of caution:

1. **Establish selection criteria**
   Have some objective standard to determine if someone is eligible for enshrinement on your wall. If it just happens at the whim of the manager or someone on the staff, it becomes a game of favorites and has no importance.

2. **Don't surprise anyone**
   Be sure you have the person's permission before you consign them to immortality. If people

58

prefer not to have their picture posted, respect their wishes.

3. Make it an event
To make enshrinement truly an honor, treat it as such. At the least, the honoree should invite their friends to witness the enshrinement.

Hold the ceremony on a slow night. You can use the business and there will be fewer distractions that can pull your attention away from the person being honored.

Precede the unveiling with a short testimonial (serious or otherwise) about the person being honored and what they did to merit the honor being bestowed. Their picture, whether a photo or a caricature, should be professionally done and presented in a frame of appropriate quality.

4. Hold a ceremony.
Enshrinement is even more powerful if there is a little ceremony that goes along with the honor. Come up with something that will be memorable, fun, not (too) embarrassing to the participants and which will bring you in a little money in the process!

Just so things aren't too one-sided, you might want to make a contribution to the honoree's charity of choice. Who knows? Just use your imagination and you will be fine.

Living large
My colleague, Max Hitchins, owns Billy the Pigs Pub in Sydney, Australia.

When you become one of the regulars at Billy's, Max has your picture actually painted onto the wall of the place! He has a spectacular group mural that is constantly being expanded with new faces. He even has the faces of his regulars painted onto the support columns in the bar.

Do you think that might make someone feel rather special? Do you think they might come in more often and bring their friends?

19

Send thank-you notes

Did you ever receive a thank-you note after you dined at a restaurant for the first time or hosted a small group dinner? If you did, would you consider it a special gesture? Would you be more likely to go back to the restaurant again?

This doesn't need to be anything more than a simple "Thank you for coming in and I hope to see you again soon" note, handwritten, of course.

Perhaps this is just another way to show gratitude, but a thank-you note is a tangible expression that shows guests they are important to you and that you appreciate their patronage.

You may have the diner's name from the credit card. If you have a phone number from the reservation list, you can find their address in a reverse telephone directory. They may have signed up for your frequent diner plan. There are many ways to get a guest's address if you really want it.

Use this idea with care, particularly with couples – you don't want to risk embarrassing anyone. One restaurant I know only sends notes to parties of four or more for this very reason.

Certainly, someone who hosts a dinner for eight or more deserves a personal thank-you from the management, but how about a note from the server as well? After all, that is the strongest point of connection for most folks.

A personal note can be a very effective way to develop a personal connection (assuming that nothing went drastically wrong while the guest was in the restaurant) . . . provided that the manager and the server made a personal connection with the guests during the meal and provided the note truly comes from the heart!

20

Do a better job with birthdays

What do you do when someone celebrates a birthday in your restaurant – sing a lame version of "Happy Birthday to You?"

(The only thing worse, in my opinion, is that stupid "Happy, Happy Birthday" song complete with half-hearted hand-clapping from a group of brain-dead servers who clearly would rather be elsewhere and who can't wait for it to be over. It only disrupts your other diners and irritates the celebrant.)

If you want to create a connection and become "the place to go" to celebrate a birthday, you have to do better than that. After all, you may see several birthdays a night and may handle them virtually on "automatic," but your guest only has one birthday a year and it is important to them.

Be unique
You don't necessarily have to be wild and crazy, but you can certainly develop a unique approach to acknowledging a birthday.

When you celebrate a birthday at one of the Azteca Mexican Restaurants in the northwest, first they plop a big, dumb sombrero on your head (there is no other way to adequately describe it!) Naturally, you are grinning like a fool at this point.

That is the moment they take a Polaroid snapshot and sing a birthday song (in Spanish, of course!) Your photo goes into a little paper frame that is then signed by all the members of the staff. Happy Birthday from your amigos at Azteca!

Give 'em
At the least, offer a free cake to guests celebrating a birthday or anniversary.

You know that there are people who will take advantage of you and request a cake when it not really their birthday. You may have even done it yourself once or twice. People like this love to get away with something . . . but they typically have several people with them and all are paying full price for dinner. Go ahead. Take advantage of me!

64

Celebrating with style and grace

For small upscale operations, there is an alternative to the often-annoying practice of singing to guests.

Rap on a glass to get the attention of the room and propose a toast. "To Mickey and Sylvia on the occasion of their thirtieth anniversary. May you have another 30 years together!"

Everyone raises their glasses, acknowledges the couple, drinks a little and the deed is neatly done.

21

Get the kids involved

While in Tampa recently, a group of us went to dinner at Tuscan Oven, a country Italian restaurant (wood-fired oven, display cooking – great place!)

One member of the party brought his family along, including his 5-year-old son who, naturally, wanted a pizza. The waitress brought the rolled out dough, sauce, cheese and pepperoni. The child made his own pizza . . . right at the table!

The staff took it back to the oven and the child watched as they baked it for him. Talk about thrilled! He even insisted on taking home all of the leftovers of HIS PIZZA!

How can you adapt this idea?

22

Hold a
guest appreciation dinner

Did a restaurant ever invite you to be their guest for a dinner in your honor? If you know David Duthie, it could happen! David owns a restaurant called The Yellow Brick Toad in Lambertville, New Jersey and does a superb job of guest recognition.

Every year he holds a special Guest Appreciation dinner for his regulars, the highlight of which is the announcement of his "Patron of the Year" who is then enshrined with a cast brass plaque on the restaurant wall.

In addition to the annual honor, David also gives out other awards at this event.

67

His restaurant actively supports local charities, so he regularly encourages his guests to volunteer to help with a variety of community activities over the course of the year.

At the annual banquet, he gives out "Being There" awards to those people who helped by "being there" when they were needed.

How could you adapt an idea like this?

23

Buy regular guests a bottle of wine

Let's say that you own a place called "Benny's Diner" – a "Mom and Pop" joint with a regular eggs and coffee morning crowd and a modest check average – a place that sees the same regulars almost every day of the week. You want to make sure these valued guests know that you appreciate their patronage by doing something special to acknowledge the special events in their lives.

You would certainly invite your guests for a special deal sometime during the month of their birthday or anniversary. You might even send them a coupon they could use anytime at their convenience. After all, you want to keep them coming back.

69

You also know that your restaurant will probably not be an appropriate dining choice when they celebrate their tenth wedding anniversary!

But if the celebrants were regular patrons and you were serious about letting them know how much you appreciate their business, you would find out where they intended to go on the special day itself.

Picture this scene: They sit down to a beautiful dinner at "La Splendido." The lighting is romantic, the music is soft, the glassware sparkles and the promise of a memorable meal is in the air.

The waiter comes to the table, and presents a bottle of wine (or complimentary desserts) along with a card signed by all the staff of your restaurant saying, "Best wishes for a happy anniversary from your friends at Benny's Diner!"

Would that have impact? As the couple celebrates their anniversary in a competitor's restaurant, my guess is that they will be talking about the incredible people at Benny's Diner!

What I am suggesting is an intensely personal gesture – a gift with no immediate benefit to the giver – and they will love it! What do you bet that they will return to Benny's to say thank you? That one visit alone will pay for the cost of the wine.

Better yet, the gesture will create a more personal connection with Benny's Diner and further solidify the long-term relationship.

Even if you do not buy a gift, what would it take to send a card, signed by everyone on the staff, to acknowledge the special occasion?

Part 4

Be Guest-Friendly

24
No unhappy guests

The high-tech, cutting edge secret to making big bucks in the hospitality business is no more complicated than this: *no unhappy guests!*

The only reason your restaurant exists is to make sure that the people you serve are thrilled by what you do for them.

If you have people walking out the door, and they are not excited about what happened inside your four walls, you are in big trouble!

None of us operate in a market that is so big that we can afford to let *anyone* get away!

When I was first managing restaurants, I knew that making the guests happy was one of the things I wanted to do, but it was on the list with getting the ice machine fixed, trying to cover Karen's shift this weekend and all the other things that end up in the typical manager's pile.

It was not until relatively recently that it hit me on a very gut level that making the guests happy is the only real job we have. Until, and unless, the guests are happy, nothing else really matters.

In fact, making the guests happy is the "litmus test" for everything we do in the hospitality business:

- Should you buy that new piece of equipment? It makes sense if having it will help make sure the guests are happy.

- Should you allocate more time and money to staff training? Unless you think that untrained staff can make your guests happy, training is a good thing.

- Should you hire a "warm body" to fill a vacancy? If you believe you can make the guests happy with substandard workers, have at it. (It never works, by the way.)

If you are passionately committed to making sure your guests have a great time every time they dine with you, sales cannot help but increase.

25

Of course we can!

That is the answer to the question. Which question, you ask? **Any** question you get from a guest, most questions that you get from your staff . . . and even the majority of those tricky questions that you ask yourself!

The phrase pays homage to "Coach" Don Smith's credo, "The answer is yes. What's the question?" but it takes the idea a bit farther.

You want to make your guests happy (which will never happen when you tell them what you **can't** do for them!) And, since your staff will treat your guests the same way you treat your staff, it is not a good precedent to start saying no to them, either.

You can probably understand this idea in the context of dealing with guests and staff, but how often do you stop yourself from moving to the next level, either personally or professionally, by just automatically thinking that you cannot do it?

- Increase sales by 20%? Of course we can!
- Cut turnover by 50%? Of course we can!
- Get guests to come back one more time a month? Of course we can!
- Have a life? Of course we can!

The way to accomplish these goals will not always be immediately obvious – in most cases it will not be – but by first applying "the answer" and worrying about the details later, you will be amazed at the possibilities you will suddenly start to see.

If you want to eliminate most guest relations problems before they start, I suggest you adopt this simple management philosophy. It will force you to find ways to say "yes" rather than simply accepting an easy "no."

This attitude keeps the emphasis on assuring that guests have an enjoyable experience every time they dine in your restaurant. It will cause your guests to want to return more often.

It just makes hospitality sense.

26
Resolve complaints quickly

Unlike fine wine, complaints do not get better with age. A minor inconvenience can become a full-blown crisis (at least to the guest) if left unattended.

Based on a survey by the National Retail Merchants Association, 14% of the people who stop patronizing a business do so because they had a complaint that was not handled well. That is a lot of business to give away due to lack of skill and understanding when it comes to dealing with guest complaints.

Statistics reveal that seven out of ten complaining guests will do business with you again if you resolve the complaint *in their favor*. Complaints do not resolve in any way other than in favor of the guest.

79

Research also suggests if you resolve a complaint on the spot, 95% of complaining guests will do business with you again . . . and the only people on the spot are typically your service staff. If you need a case to give your crew the authority to do what they have to do at the table at the time, this is the case – 95% guest retention vs. 70% retention.

Act quickly

A pro will notice (and correct) minor annoyances before they have a chance to grow into complaints. If you sense that a guest is not delighted, make it right – right now. No excuses, no hassles.

If you have an upset guest, you must address the upset and not the circumstances behind it. It is not important why they are upset – it may not even have anything to do with the restaurant or with you, but make it right anyway.

Never negotiate a guest's complaint. The only approach that will work is to apologize for the situation and fix it immediately.

The good news

It appears that if someone has a complaint that is handled well, they are more loyal than if they never had a complaint at all.

I do not propose that you make mistakes just so you can fix them – errors will happen without any

80

special effort – but handling a complaint well is a personal statement of caring that establishes a more personal connection between the guest and your restaurant.

Remember that you are not just solving a problem, you are making an investment in securing a regular patron. The cost of keeping a guest is always less than the cost of losing one.

If guests do not have a good memory of their visit, they won't come back and that will be a huge blow to everyone's income!

27

Offer an escort to the car

Seniors, especially women, have concern for their personal safety. They appreciate an escort to their cars in the evening. By being sensitive to this fear, you can endear yourself to elderly patrons.

If you choose to offer this service, give official notice of your offer. Seniors are more comfortable if the offer of assistance is made by someone they know, like a manager or a hostess, and they are suspicious of strangers who offer to help.

If possible, have escorts wear your restaurant's uniform. It will help put elderly guests more at ease.

28
Make it easy for large groups

Going out to eat with a large group of people can be a hassle. It is particularly awkward when the party first sits down and everyone is getting settled. If the meal gets off to a good start, it is likely to be more fun for everyone!

Train your service staff to immediately recommend a selection of appetizers for the group to share. At least a few of the items should be ones you can get out of the kitchen quickly.

Find out if they want separate checks and if they do, offer to divide the cost of the appetizers equally between the diners.

If they don't want appetizers, bring bread or
something else to nibble on. Get some beverages
on the table fast.

Make it easier and more pleasant for the group and
they will have a better memory of your place and be
more likely to return.

29

Allow for the needs of blind patrons

Braille menus

If a guest spoke another language, you would try to get someone who could translate, wouldn't you? Why not extend the same courtesy to blind guests?

Most towns have a local agency who provides services for the blind. Ask them to translate your menu to Braille.

Menus on tape

The Americans With Disabilities Act says that we either have to have menus in Braille or have a staff member read the menu to a blind patron.

A blind friend told me that only about 10% of blind people read Braille and it is difficult to break a server loose long enough to read the menu when most operations are running short-handed to begin with.

A seminar attendee had a wonderful solution to this dilemma – she records her menu on a Walkman-type tape player. This allows the blind diner to go through the menu at their own pace and makes it easier to provide the "word pictures" that a good server would paint of the menu items.

An added benefit is that the menu is much easier to update than a Braille version would be.

"Would you like the chef to cut the meat?"
This is a polite way to offer assistance to a blind patron without being condescending. It lets a blind diner off the hook when they order an item, such as steak, that will need to be cut. Better yet, it does it without risk of giving the impression that you think the diner is incapable of fending for himself.

30

On-time reservations

Guests make reservations at 7:00pm because they want to eat at 7:00pm. Whenever you accept a reservation and keep guests waiting, you run the risk of losing them forever.

You have a few minutes of grace but people will not be pleased if they have to wait very long. Your job is to find a way to operate that allows you to keep your tables full and still honor reservations on time.

Often, we are our own worst enemies in this regard because we take reservations for every table in the house. It may make you feel good to look at a full reservations book, but I think it is just a disaster waiting to happen. Here is the problem:

When every table is tightly scheduled, a party that "camps" longer than expected has a domino effect on the flow of business for the rest of the night. It puts you in a position of making people wait, often for quite awhile, after you had promised to seat them at a certain time.

It is not your fault that the first party ran long, but it is still your responsibility to make things work for all your guests.

The safest policy is to always have a percentage of your tables that you do not reserve. This gives you a buffer and a spot for walk-in business. If a table hangs on longer than expected, seat the waiting reservation at one of the unreserved tables, even if it means making the walk-in party wait a little longer.

Get your points
As you are seating guests (on time!), be sure to remind them that at your restaurant, 7:00 means 7:00. They will remember that the next time they go to a competitor and are left stewing in the bar.

One more idea: how about adopting a policy that if you cannot seat people within three minutes of their reservation time, you will buy them a round of appetizers and their drinks will be free until you can get them to the table? That will keep your feet to the fire and help keep the guests happy which will, in turn, make them want to come back more often.

31

Provide armchairs for elderly diners

As people get older, their bodies become more fragile. Moving about becomes a harder process and simple tasks like sitting down and standing up takes more work.

Armchairs permit older diners to use their arms to get in and out of the chairs, making the process much easier. If all your chairs have arms, you are already elder-friendly.

If not all your chairs have arms, moving armchairs to the table before the older guests are seated (and letting them know that you did it just for them) is a delightful touch!

32

Provide diaper-changing tables (in both restrooms)

When diapers have to be changed, diapers will be changed. I have seen it done on the table in the dining room! Even the counter at the restroom sink is not a particularly desirable location.

Diaper-changing tables are wall-mounted to save space. When you install changing tables, be sure to put one in the men's room as well and include a separate, covered container for the soiled diapers or they will be flushed down the toilet and clog up your plumbing!

I like this idea: A seminar attendee said that she mounted the changing table on the wall in the disabled stall where there is almost always a solid wall and a little more room. This has several advantages:

As one Mom told me, "When I go into the restroom with my child, I have business to take care of as well. It is nice to be able to close the stall door and corral the little guy."

The other plus is that when diapers are changed, they are changed out of sight, a pleasant relief for your other guests as well.

One other suggestion to make your restaurant more baby-friendly: keep a stock of disposable diapers (in assorted sizes) on hand and post a sign in the restrooms to let people know.

Most parents come prepared, but if an emergency arises, it's hard to improvise. You will gain points for attention to detail even if they never take advantage of the offer.

33

Get permission before refilling coffee or tea

Do you take cream and sugar in your coffee?

If you drink coffee any way but black, you know that everyone has a certain "perfect" balance of coffee, cream and sugar.

It is annoying to get the coffee fixed just the way you like it and then have some jerk top off the cup and throw the whole chemistry off! The same holds true for iced tea or any other beverage that the diner may "doctor up" to taste.

If you refill the cup without permission, you upset that balance and risk irritating the guest.

Just ask permission before you pour the refill and you will stand out from most of your competitors.

This does not require any extended conversation. Just train the servers to come to the table, pause and try to make eye contact before automatically swooping in to refill the coffee or tea.

If the guest has it the way they want it, this will give them time to let you know it, often just by holding a hand over the top of the cup or glass.

Be sure, too, that guests always know when you have refilled a cup with hot coffee. People can space out anything and you don't want an accidental scalding because a diner didn't notice that you added hot coffee to a cup they expected to be cooler!

34

Adjust the appetizer
to the size of the party

This is an unexpected personal touch that is so easy
to do, yet few operators ever think to accommodate
or suggest it.

Let's say you have a party of four who order an
appetizer that normally comes with three pieces.
What would it take to offer to size it for four people,
add an extra piece and adjust the price accordingly?

Whatever it takes, it is worth the effort to make your
restaurant more guest-friendly. Besides, it is the
personal awareness and concern for the guests
inherent in the offer that will delight your diners.

35

Bring a fresh cup of coffee

Sometimes the guest orders coffee and the half-full cup just sits on the table for a while. Once coffee is cold, the best that topping it off will do is to bring the coffee temperature to somewhere around lukewarm!

If a partially-full cup has been sitting for a while, either bring the diner a full cup of hot coffee or bring a clean cup and fill it at the table.

This may present a chance for you to educate the guest as to what you are doing for them (remember what we said about word-of-mouth) and help them be aware of the extra service you are providing.

This simple gesture will assure the guest will have a hot, satisfying cup of coffee and you will have demonstrated how much you care.

Both will work to your benefit when it comes time for them to figure the tip or decide whether or not to return!

Part 5

Give Guests Something to Talk About

36

Understand how word-of-mouth works

Word-of-mouth may be the best advertising, but there can be no word-of-mouth without something to talk about!

If you want guests to tell their friends about your place (and if you want them to come back more often), you have to educate them as to why they come to your restaurant in the first place.

The basic premise of word-of-mouth is that people like to know things that other people don't know.

- When your staff knows things that your guests don't know, they will tell your guests about them.

99

- When your guests know things that their friends don't know, they will tell their friends about them.

If you want it to happen, you have to make it happen. This suggests that word-of-mouth really starts with educating your staff about what you have, what you do, why you do it that way and what makes it better or different from what your competitors offer.

Is this important? Talking power aside for the moment, if you cannot create points of difference, you must compete strictly on the basis of price.

Do you want to compete on price? If you could not make a distinction in your mind between a Yugo and a Mercedes Benz, why would you pay $60,000 for a car?

37

Educate guests as to why they dine with you

This is not meant as an indictment, but most people are relatively unsure of themselves.

To counter insecurity, or perhaps just because our minds seem to work this way, we need reasons to justify their decisions ("I do this because . . .").

Think about it. If someone asked why you drive the particular car you do, your response would likely begin, "I drive a _____ because . . ." You are not likely to say, "Gee, I never thought about it!"

If you want guests to patronize your operation more often – and remember that the safe route to the big bucks is just to get current guests back just one additional time each month – then they need reasons to justify their increased patronage.

In other words, you have to educate your guests so that they will know why they dine with you. The rationale is still "I go there because . . ."

Your mission is to fill in the blank for your guests – to be sure they know why they come to you so they will have the justification they need to continue to do it!

So if you want guests to talk about you, it's not enough that they had a good time – in order to talk they need to know **why** they had a good time.

Are you telling them?

38
Offer free _____ if guests have to wait

The first Pacific Café opened in San Francisco in the late 70s. It was out toward the beach – not a particularly prime location – and the weather was often cold and foggy. It was a small restaurant and had no place inside for guests to wait.

One night shortly after they opened, there was a line of waiting diners extending down the sidewalk. Feeling sorry that his guests had to wait in the cold, the manager offered free wine to everyone until they could be seated.

Needless to say, the waiting patrons loved it and didn't mind the wait nearly as much!

103

The word spread quickly. The next night there was another line. The manager gave away more wine and a tradition was established. The waiting line (and the complimentary wine) continue to this day. The restaurant has given away a lot of wine . . . and they have also sold a lot of dinners!

(I suspect that somewhere there is an accountant going crazy over all the money spent on free wine. The restaurant has had a line out the door for more than 20 years. I don't think they care!)

I told this story at the Virginia Restaurant Show several years ago and later heard how one of the attendees applied the idea.

He had a restaurant on "the strip" in Richmond with all his competitors lined up next to him. Valentine's Day that year fell on a Friday night, so he knew that V-Day was going to be particularly busy.

Recalling the Pacific Café story, he bought two cases of cheap champagne. When he was on a wait, he told the walk-ins that the champagne was on him until he could seat them. He said he knew he did $4000 in business that would have walked to his competitors . . . and it cost him $60 to do it!

(Actually, I like giving away free champagne. People will have one glass and go back to ordering Scotch and water!)

It's the offer, stupid

The attraction is in the offer, not the alcohol. A case in point is Lou Mitchell's in Chicago.

If you are ever in the Windy City, make it a point to have breakfast at Lou Mitchell's. You will probably have to wait a few minutes (there has been a line at Lou Mitchell's for more than 40 years!) but when they cannot seat you immediately, they still take care of you: women get a small box of Milk Duds, men get donut holes and children get a free banana! People don't mind waiting, even in the morning.

If you can get someone's day off to a good start, you have done them a real favor. Timing is critical during the breakfast period, so anything you can do to make a delay less painful is a good move.

Even offering free coffee and a newspaper to guests who have to wait is a small gesture that will yield big returns in guest satisfaction.

The important point is that whatever offer you make is personal – let ME (as a person) do this for YOU (as a person.)

If you are just going through the motions ("OK, I guess we have a wait. Here is your stupid cup of coffee.") people will justifiably feel insulted.

105

39

Give away free meals

What? You must be thinking that I have really lost touch with reality, right? This idea may not be as insane as it sounds. Consider this:

When Phil Romano opened the first Macaroni Grill outside San Antonio, he wanted to increase dinner business early in the week. His solution was to give away all the meals on a Monday or Tuesday night!

He only did it a few times but the word quickly spread and the place was packed on Mondays and Tuesdays because "this might be the night!"

The chance for a free meal was more intriguing than a guaranteed percentage off from a coupon.

106

Do you have a period when you would like to increase business?

- How much would it cost you to give away all the meals during that period?
- How much advertising could you buy for the cost of the free meals?
- How much word-of-mouth exposure would you get if you gave away all the meals during that period?

One way to give away free meals is with a fish bowl drawing where the guest draws a slip of paper at the end of the meal to find out what they get. The first few times, be sure to have a disproportionate number of free meal tickets in the bowl.

After awhile, you can adjust the mix of rewards (free meals, free desserts, 50% off and so forth) to any ratio you want (but be sure to give away several free meals each time).

You could also just make a random management decision or give your staff the OK to comp a certain number of meals during the target meal period.

Do not advertise the policy
Whatever method you choose, do not advertise the policy. The message will be stronger when it is carried by word-of-mouth. People are reluctant to talk about an offer that is being widely advertised because it's not something that others don't know.

At the least, be sure your servers tell your guests what it is that you want your guests to tell their friends. ("Isn't this fun? We don't advertise the fact, but we do this every Monday and Tuesday night. Come back next week, you might get lucky again.")

Protect the tips
When you give away a meal, you risk costing your service staff some of their tip income, so you might want to approach the table like this: "Your dinner tonight came to $50. If you will take care of your server, I will take care of your meal."

This will let them know the value of what you did for them and help assure that the servers will not be penalized (with a lower tip) for your decision to give away the meal.

By the way, if it turns out that your servers are losing tip money due to this policy, throw a little extra money their way so they remain supportive of the program. It is the right thing to do.

40

Invest in a few restroom amenities

Although restroom amenities probably have more relevance in upscale operations, anyone can add a few pleasant surprises.

Unexpected touches like hand lotion, dispensed paper cups and complimentary packets of pain reliever (local ordinances permitting) will reflect your concern.

Consider a selection of aftershave lotions in the men's room. Amenities like a magnifying makeup mirror, a couch or flowers in the ladies' room can make a big impression.

What if a guest needs to blow their nose, wipe off some makeup or do other little odd jobs? In most places, the choice is only paper towels or toilet paper – not really much of a choice!

Follow the example of most hotels and install a dispenser of tissues. Facial tissue is an inexpensive small touch that creates another point of difference from your competition.

If you have the wall space, how about a full length mirror in each restroom? Many people like to check their appearance before returning to the dining room or lounge. If they can see themselves fully, there is less chance they might be embarrassed by a detail they couldn't see in the mirror over the sink.

Fresh flowers in the ladies' room, totally in keeping with the tone of an upscale restaurant, might not be appropriate in a coffee shop. Still, a small vase of dried flowers on the counter could work.

Pictures on the walls or interesting light fixtures help avoid the institutional feel. If it makes your guests feel more comfortable, it is worth considering.

Restrooms also can make a statement. Consider the Madonna Inn in San Luis Obispo, California where they give tours of the men's room! Could it be something about having a 9-foot waterfall over natural rocks instead of more traditional urinals?

110

Have you heard about the 300-lb. blocks of ice they used to put in the oversized urinals at P.J. Clarke's in New York City? The practice is more than 100 years old (it was the preferred sanitation method before chemicals) and gives PJ's a clear point of difference in the market.

The ladies' room at the Drake Hotel in Chicago is really several private rooms. Behind a full-length door, you have your own toilet, sink, mirror and stool – it is your room!

You could do worse than being known for having the greatest ladies' room in town!

People expect restrooms to be utilitarian, so style is an unexpected surprise! Give the same attention to the decor of the restrooms as you do to decorating your restaurant and you will be amazed at the compliments you will receive!

41

Provide stuffed animals to "dine" with the kids

The Family Buggy in Livonia, Michigan has several large stuffed bears. When there are children at the table, they pull up an extra chair and bring over one of the bears to "dine" with the children.

They started with one, immediately had to get a second and probably have a third and fourth one by now. The kids are excited and the restaurant has a point of difference from competitors.

They also sell the bears . . . to the grandparents . . . for $200 each!

42

Put in a Lego® table and play area

Kids love Legos® or other similar building blocks. If you have an unproductive corner of the dining room, perhaps one with a "bad table" that irritates guests when they are seated there, de everyone a favor and convert it into a play area for small children.

The play area itself is delightful and the Lego® table is an easy way to occupy children in (relatively) quiet activity. It will also set you apart from competitors who only offer coloring books.

43

Provide a toy box

I know several restaurants who have a toy box at the entrance. Children are allowed to select one toy from the box each time they come in. It is theirs to play with until they leave. If they want to play with another toy, they can do it the next time they return.

You can either purchase toys or collect them from your other diners, many of whom probably have a garage full of playthings from children long since grown – a great way to tie the older crowd a little closer to your operation.

If you know a child has a particular favorite, you could let them reserve it when their parents make the dinner reservation!

44

Schedule occasional "front door" deliveries

Picture Newport, Rhode Island in the summer. It is 5:30pm at the height of the tourist season and the popular restaurant is already packed with hungry guests waiting for dinner.

The fish delivery is late. By the time the driver gets to the restaurant, he can barely find a place to stop, let alone get his truck around back to the kitchen, so he double-parks in front. He finds the manager and asks her what she wants to do about the 90-pound tuna he has in the truck.

The manager thinks for a second and then, with a sly smile, says "Bring it in through the front door!"

115

Now picture two deliverymen, holding this huge fish above their heads as they weave their way through the crowd and disappear into the kitchen!

Do you think people will talk about it? Do you think the guests will get the idea that the tuna is fresh? You bet!

This is not appropriate for everything you order – boxes of portion cut beef wrapped in Cryovac, for example, are not particularly visual! But if you have a product with strong eye appeal, consider putting it on display rather than hiding it.

I know one college bar that always has its beer delivered through the front door. You can imagine how the sight of endless kegs rolling through the crowd strikes joy into the hearts of college students!

45

Offer free postcards

Are you in a resort area? If so, print up some great postcards featuring a photo of your restaurant on the front, then offer the cards (for free!) To guests who are waiting for tables.

If they are on vacation, they will have the obligatory "wish you were here" cards to send so why not have them send out ads for your restaurant? While they are waiting, they can take care of their social obligations and the time will pass more quickly.

If you want to make it particularly delightful, offer to mail the cards for them. Stamps are less expensive (and personal endorsements are more powerful) than display ads.

46

Provide a selection of reading glasses

It's hell when you pass 40!

For your guests who need a little optical help and have forgotten their reading glasses, why not have a selection on hand to help them out?

Reading glasses in standard prescriptions are readily available in most pharmacies. Present the selection in a good-looking lined wooden box.

Your guests will appreciate and remember this unexpected amenity. It will also be something they can talk to their friends about!

47

Have a selection of sunglasses on the deck

When the weather is good, seating on an outside deck is a treat. The problem is that intense sun can make it an eye-straining experience.

Why not have a box of sunglasses to lend to diners on the deck? The cost is minimal and the offer of some sun protection is an unexpected surprise.

My second restaurant had a great deck. The loaner sunglasses were a big hit and we also found that many guests forgot their sunglasses anyway and never bothered returning for them. When that happened, we just added them to the box!

48

Do something unexpected

A McGuffey's Restaurant in North Carolina had a problem: there was construction going on next to the restaurant and the guests' cars were getting covered with dust.

The management had some time on their hands one slow afternoon, so on a whim, they decided to wash the cars in the parking lot while their diners were having lunch!

The guests were thrilled! The next week, they did it again and again received raves. After that, they washed all the cars in the lot on Monday afternoons . . . and Monday soon became the second busiest lunch of the week!

Can you imagine how much goodwill you would create by an unexpected gesture like this?

What is the potential for taking the sting out of waiting in line at a quick service drive-up window by washing guests' cars? You could even have a school group do the work as a fund raiser except that **you** pay them for each car washed, not the guest.

You could even make a few points just by cleaning windshields!

These ideas work because they were spontaneous responses to a guest need and came from a genuine desire to delight others. If they are applied as a technique, they will fall flat.

You will be amazed at the goodwill you can create when you are open to these opportunities and take action in the interest of delighting your guests.

Part 6

Differentiate Yourself from Other Restaurants

49

Differentiate the basics

While it is definitely to your advantage to create elements and products that are unique to your operation, it is also important to create points of difference in those items you know that every other restaurant offers.

If you are successful in this regard, you will give guests reasons to think of you every time they dine elsewhere.

So what does every restaurant offer? Let's start with items like water, napkins, coffee, soft drinks, beer, wine, salad, bread, restrooms and telephones.

In general, you can create a point of difference in

125

any of these items either in the product itself, the way it is presented or any policies you might have with regard to it.

Here are some ideas to get you started thinking how you might be able to exploit these differences to your advantage:

	Product	Presentation/Policy
Water	local spring water imported water bottled water specially filtered water	pressed glass bottle carafe service flower petal in the glass
Napkins	oversized different material (calico, towel)	napkin rings hot towels before or after the meal
Coffee	special blend flavored coffees espresso and cappuccino	oversized or crested mugs carafe service brewed at the table
Soft drinks	bottled vs. post mix extensive selection brewed root beer	free refills carafe service
Beer	extensive micro brews extensive imports local/regional brews	unusual glassware personalized mugs bottles served in a bucket of ice
Salad	unusual ingredients exceptionally chilled house made dressings	unusual salad bowls oversized bowls

Wine	little-known vineyards extensive wine list moderate pricing policy	oversized glasses higher quality glassware for upper end wines pouring house wine at the table
Bread	exceptional, piping hot bread drop biscuits quick breads	individual cutting boards on sheet pans hot from the oven
Restrooms	dual restrooms (2 for men, 2 for women vs. one of each) over-fixturing and extra space	amenities panic button ice in the urinals
Telephones	sound effects panel foreign phone booth unusual privacy	free notepads free local calls tableside phones

Any good thing can be overdone. It probably goes without saying, but as you start to add elements to differentiate your operation, keep the bigger picture in mind.

Any of these distinctions can help set one operation apart from another but not all of them are appropriate for every restaurant.

127

50

Use oversized wine glasses

There is something elegant about a large wine glass that makes people feel more like ordering wine.

When I had my first restaurant in San Francisco in the late 70's, white wine was the drink of choice. All my competitors were serving nine ounces of wine in a ten-ounce glass.

We served ten ounces of wine in a seventeen-ounce glass and promptly gained the patronage of most of the women in the Financial District! They loved the look and feel of the big glass.

We also had less spillage while carrying drinks to the table through a crowded bar.

128

By using a different presentation (the oversized glass), we sold ten ounces of wine for 25% more than our competitors were getting for nine ounces! Better yet, we set ourselves apart from others in the market, had stronger word-of-mouth and created happier guests in the process!

The larceny factor
You may have a concern that guests will steal your nice, big wine glasses. They will! We lost a lot of them.

If I was doing it all over again, the only change I would make is to put my logo on the glasses. That way, the "thief" would be more certain to think of me every time he poured a glass of wine in his apartment!

51

Offer wines based on consumption

I was delighted when I first saw this idea at Le Central in Denver. Billed as "the affordable French restaurant," Le Central will sell you wine by the glass and they will sell you wine by the taste.

I had seen both those formats before, but it was the first time I had seen a restaurant that sold wine based on the percentage of the bottle that you consumed!

I questioned the idea initially, but I could not see a health department problem unless a guest drank from the bottle! The more I thought about it, the more I liked the idea.

130

A glass of wine is a lot for my wife (and finishing the rest of the bottle is less fun for me than it used to be), so a whole bottle is often just too much for the two of us.

On the other hand, when we are out with another couple, one bottle is not quite enough. I never liked getting caught in the "do we or don't we" debate on ordering a second bottle.

This policy avoids both problems . . . and makes your bottle of Mondavi different from the same bottle at your competitor's.

You might want to keep control of the bottle and your liquor laws may or may not address this issue, but this is an idea worth considering, particularly if no one else in your market is doing it yet.

52

Serve bottles of beer in a bucket of ice

I first saw this idea in Mexico and I like it.

Any beer drinker knows that the only way to have an ice cold beer is to chill the beer on ice. For reasons I still do not totally understand, beer chilled in a refrigerator just never tastes as cold.

The bucket is a perfect way to keep the unpoured beer cold until the guest is ready to drink it . . . and to differentiate yourself from your competitors.

How else can you make your bottle of Budweiser different from anyone else's bottle of Bud?

53

Establish signature items

What are you famous for? What do I absolutely have to try when I come to your restaurant? What item do you do better than anyone else in town? What can I get in your restaurant that I cannot get anywhere else?

The answer to these questions will identify your signature items. If you are not already famous for something, **declare** yourself famous for something!

Certainly you should have a signature entree but how about a signature appetizer, a signature salad, a signature bread and a signature dessert? Do you have a signature before-dinner drink, a signature after-dinner drink and a signature coffee?

How about a signature side dish? Tadich Grill, the oldest restaurant in San Francisco, is as known among the locals for their creamed spinach as for their fresh fish.

Somebody in town will have a reputation for the best onion rings, the best fried zucchini or the best hash browns. Why couldn't it be you?

Signatures do not even have to be an all-the-time thing – you can have seasonal signatures.

How about a "special winter slaw" that you only serve in January and February (when, just by "coincidence," lettuce quality is in the basement and the price is through the roof)?

Your staff and your guests will ultimately identify your best items. In fact, your signatures may turn out to be items other than the ones you thought they would be. Don't let that bother you.

Once your signature items are identified, make sure they are noted as such on your menu. When a guest opens the menu, it should be clear which items you want them to order.

"I go there because . . ."

54

Offer a selection of local or regional beverages

As a continual traveler, I always appreciate the chance to sample regional specialties.

The boom in micro breweries has re-energized the beer market and more regions of the country are discovering that they can produce wines of reasonable quality. Even draft root beer is a nice change from mass market soft drinks.

Educating guests to the unique regional products can make the evening more memorable and help support local producers.

55

Offer smaller portions
at smaller prices

Dieters and elderly diners particularly appreciate this
option and it can work to your advantage.

You can offer half the portion for 60-75% of the
menu price and still maintain respectable margins.
It is less about the price and more about the fact
that many people just don't want that much food.

This approach allows entrees to be attractive as
appetizers. Guests can sample a wider range of
your entrees without having to commit to a full
portion of anything. Half portions also make you
more attractive to the growing number of diners
who prefer grazing to ordering a full meal.

136

56

Give guests "something for nothing"

Earlier, I mentioned Lou Mitchell's in Chicago because they give you something if you have to wait. That is not the entire story.

When you get seated, they bring you some fresh fruit that you didn't order. Halfway through breakfast, you get some frozen yogurt with fresh strawberries – a palate cleanser . . . at breakfast! The bread is baked on premises and they have a special filtered water to brew their coffee.

Lou Mitchell's food is well-prepared and reasonably priced, but I think a large measure of their success has to do with these little unexpected extras.

137

At Lambert's Café in Sikeston, Missouri, waiters are continuously bringing buckets of hot food you did not order and adding it to the already heaping portions on your plate.

The white beans, macaroni and tomatoes, fried okra, red pepper relish, slaw, fried potatoes, cooked apples and rolls bigger than softballs are all extra . . . but no charge! They call them "pass-arounds" and the guests love it!

Now we know there is really nothing for nothing, but just add a few cents to your cost of goods when calculating menu prices and work the "freebies" into your cost structure. Think of it as an investment in guest delight.

Giving guests something they didn't expect – for no added charge – is definitely something that can set you apart from your penny-pinching competitors.

57

Engage in unexpected service methods

Lambert's Café is famous for "throwed rolls."

Here's how it started, as reported in an article from the Memphis Commercial Appeal newspaper:

> James Arness, Elvis and Clint Eastwood have all chowed down at Lambert's Café. And if Eastwood had said, "Make my day," or for that matter, "Kiss my foot," somebody would have thrown a roll at him. Rest assured.
>
> That's what Lambert's is famous for. "Throwed rolls."
>
> Owner Norman Lambert and the rest of the waiters throw rolls at everybody, not discriminating for age, sex, creed, color or celebrity.

139

On May 26, 1976, Norman was pushing a card of his popular homemade rolls around the dining room and a customer got impatient for service. "Throw me one," the customer said.

Norman did. He liked it. The customer liked it. The cash register liked it.

Soon Norman was perfecting his pitch and hefting hot rolls all over the place. The television and newspapers picked up on it. Reporters are always anxious for what's known affectionately in the trade as a "lite-n-brite," some catchy something for tense Dan Rather to smile about at the end of his telecast. So the reporters wrote and talked about it.

And soon people started driving from miles around to get food thrown at them. Norman's pitch became his pitch. Home of the "throwed roll" became his slogan. The little café that Norman's father and mother started on a $1,500 loan in 1942 became regionally famous. It outgrew its nine stools and eight tables and strictly local emphasis.

I won't suggest that you start tossing rolls around your dining room – in fact, you would be foolish to try it since that is Lambert's "thing" – but see if you can find some noteworthy ways to serve.

Mike Hurst ties a few helium balloons to an order of his flying fish appetizer and "flies" it to your table.

All it takes is a sense of showmanship along with a willingness (and desire) to stand out from the herd. No risk, no reward.

140

58

Garnish the doggy bag

Be proud of your food and treat it with respect. If you pack your guests' leftovers for them to take home, give it the same care and attention you give everything you do for them.

Unless your local health department prohibits it, always pack up leftovers in the kitchen, never at the table. It is difficult to load a take home container in an appetizing manner at the table.

Arrange the food attractively and then add something the guests didn't expect. It could be a garnish, extra sauce on the pasta or a container of tortilla chips with the Mexican leftovers, but it will "knock their socks off" when your guests get home!

59

Offer regional menu items made with local ingredients

In an age of homogenization, when every mall in the country has the same stores and the same chain restaurants appear on every corner, I believe there is an untapped longing for something honest.

What can you offer that people cannot get anywhere else in the country?

Lettuce from the farm down the road will always taste better than lettuce from the supermarket (but only if you let the guests know that you have used it). Find items with "talking power" and add them to your menu. It will make everyone's experience a lot more fun.

59½
The best idea of all

When it comes to building volume from your existing customers, simply remember that:

Guests come back . . . because they WANT to!

This means that to build volume, you must create (and sustain) a compelling experience for the guest, one that they will want to repeat. "If you build it, they will come" only works in the movies. To create loyal raving fans who can't wait to return and can't wait to tell their friends about you takes vision, desire and concerted action.

So this principle represents the first half of an idea. If it is going to pay off, it requires that you find ways to supply the other half. Are you up for it?

143

Appendix

Bill Marvin
The Restaurant Doctor™

Bill Marvin works with companies that want to get more done with less effort and with managers who want to get their lives back! He founded Effortless, Inc., a management research/education company and Prototype Restaurants, a hospitality consulting group.

Bill started his working life at the age of 14, washing dishes (by hand!) in a small restaurant on Cape Cod and went on to earn a degree in Hotel Administration from Cornell University. A veteran of the hospitality industry, Bill has managed hotels, institutions and clubs and owned full service restaurants.

He has had the keys in his hand, his name on the loans and the payrolls to meet. His professional curiosity and practical experience enable him to grasp (and teach) the human factors common to the growth and success of every type of service-oriented enterprise.

He is a member of the Council of Hotel and Restaurant Trainers and the National Speakers Association. He has achieved all major professional certifications in the foodservice industry. He is a prolific author and writes regular columns in the trade magazines of several industries.

In addition to a limited private consulting practice, he logs over 150,000 miles annually delivering corporate keynote addresses and conducting staff and management training programs in the United States, Canada, Europe and the Pacific Rim.

EFFORTLESS, INC.
PO Box 280 · Gig Harbor, WA 98335-0280 USA

Toll-free in North America:
Voice: (800) 767-1055 · Fax: (888) 767-1055

Local or outside North America:
Voice: (253) 858-9255 · Fax: (253) 851-6887

e-mail: bill@restaurantdoctor.com
www.restaurantdoctor.com

Reading and Resources

Here is a current summary of materials and services available from Bill Marvin and Effortless, Inc.

Books and Materials

Restaurant Basics: Why Guests Don't Come Back and What You Can Do About It, 1992, John Wiley & Sons

The Foolproof Foodservice Selection System: The Complete Manual for Creating a Quality Staff, 1993, John Wiley & Sons

From Turnover to Teamwork: How to Build and Retain a Customer-Oriented Foodservice Staff, 1994, John Wiley & Sons

50 Tips to Improve Your Tips: The Service Pro's Guide to Delighting Diners, 1995, Hospitality Masters Press

Guest-Based Marketing: How to Gain Foodservice Volume Without Losing Your Shirt, 1997, John Wiley & Sons

50 Proven Ways to Build Restaurant Sales & Profit, 1997, Hospitality Masters Press (editor and contributing author)

Cashing In On Complaints: Turning Disappointed Diners Into Gold, 1997, Hospitality Masters Press

50 Proven Ways to Enhance Guest Service, 1998, Hospitality Masters Press (editor and contributing author)

50 Proven Ways to Build More Profitable Menus, 1998, Hospitality Masters Press (editor and contributing author)

There's GOT to Be an Easier Way to Run a Business, 1999, Hospitality Masters Press

Home Remedies: A House Call from The Restaurant Doctor™, 2000, Hospitality Masters Press

More Restaurant Basics: Why Guests Don't Come Back and What You Can Do About It, 2000, Hospitality Masters Press

Bill also offers audio and video training programs, manuals and computer text files . . . and the list grows steadily. For a current catalog and price list, phone (800) 767-1055 or fax your request toll-free to (888) 767-1055. Locally or outside the US and Canada, call (253) 858-9255 or fax (253) 851-6887.

Keynotes and Seminars

Bill Marvin is generally regarded as the most-booked speaker in the hospitality industry and his messages apply equally well to any service-oriented business. No other speaker takes a similar approach to his subjects, especially in the areas of human relations and organizational effectiveness. He is also one of the few conducting training seminars for the hourly staff.

His keynotes and seminars focus on the human dimensions of hospitality, customer service, staff selection and retention. He is also in demand as a facilitator for executive retreats. When it comes to dealing with people or managing an organization, if you have ever thought, "There *has* to be an easier way to do this," schedule a house call from the Restaurant Doctor™.

Consulting Services

Bill's active speaking schedule does not leave much time for private consulting, but he is always open to an interesting offer and accepts one or two projects a year to keep his skills sharp. His expertise is in the areas of concept development/refinement and increasing sales, retention and productivity by enhancing the work climate of the company.

He has recently started one-on-one coaching with executives who want to get their lives back and deepen their understanding of how to create an organization that produces better results with less effort!

Newsletters

Bill produces "Electronic House Call," a free weekly newsletter sent by e-mail. To be placed on the EHC mailing list, send your name and e-mail address to bill@restaurantdoctor.com.

Bill also produces the bimonthly "Home Remedies" newsletter where some of the material in this book originally appeared. To receive a free six-month trial subscription, contact Bill by phone, fax or e-mail and request a sign-up form . . . or complete the sign-up form included on the following page.

A management journal for service-minded executives

Six month free trial subscription!

Home Remedies is published in January, March, May, July, September and November. The regular subscription price is only $24 a year.

❏ *Yes, sign me up!*

Please start my free trial subscription to Home Remedies newsletter.

PLEASE PRINT CLEARLY

Name _____

Company _____

Address _____

City _____ State _____ Zip _____

Phone _____ Fax _____

e-mail _____

READER INTEREST SURVEY

Information of the type below will not be included in the newsletter mailings – it will be sent ONLY to those who indicate a desire to receive it. Please indicate your level of interest: Yes (Y), No (N) or Maybe (?).

Y N ?

❏ ❏ ❏ *I am interested in knowing when you will be conducting public seminars in my part of the country.*

❏ ❏ ❏ *I am interested in hosting (or co-hosting) an in-house training program for my staff and/or managers.*

❏ ❏ ❏ *I am interested in receiving information on upcoming hospitality industry roundtables.*

❏ ❏ ❏ *I am interested in receiving information on books and materials from Bill Marvin, The Restaurant Doctor™.*

❏ ❏ ❏ *I am interested in receiving information on Bill's seminar and keynote topics.*

Return completed form to:
EFFORTLESS, INC. • PO Box 280 • Gig Harbor, WA 98335
Toll-free Fax: (888) 767-1055

Did you borrow this book? Do you want a copy of your own? Do you need extra copies for your staff and management? Do you need a great gift for a friend who runs a restaurant?

ORDER FORM

YES! I want to stretch my management thinking and add *59½ Money-Making Marketing Ideas* to my professional library.

1-9 copies: US$14.95 each
plus postage & handling

10+ copies:
call for discount information

POSTAGE & HANDLING
MUST BE ADDED TO ALL ORDERS
Figure US priority postage & handling at the greater of $5.00 vs. 6% of the total order. Orders outside the US will be sent by air mail which will be charged at cost.

No. Copies _____ **Total Amount of Order $** _____

Name _____

Company _____

Address _____

City _____ **State** ____ **Zip** _____

Phone _____ **Fax** _____

e-mail _____

Method of Payment: ❏ **Check** ❏ **VISA** ❏ **MC** ❏ **Amex** ❏ **Discover**
(For added security, credit card numbers can be faxed or phoned to Hospitality Masters Press)

Account No. _____

Expires _____ **Signature** _____

send your order to:

HOSPITALITY MASTERS PRESS
PO Box 280 • Gig Harbor, WA 98335 USA

North America toll-free Voice: (800) 767-1055
North America toll-free Fax: (888) 767-1055

Local or outside North America:
Voice: (253) 858-9255 • Fax: (253) 851-6887
e-mail: masters@harbornet.com